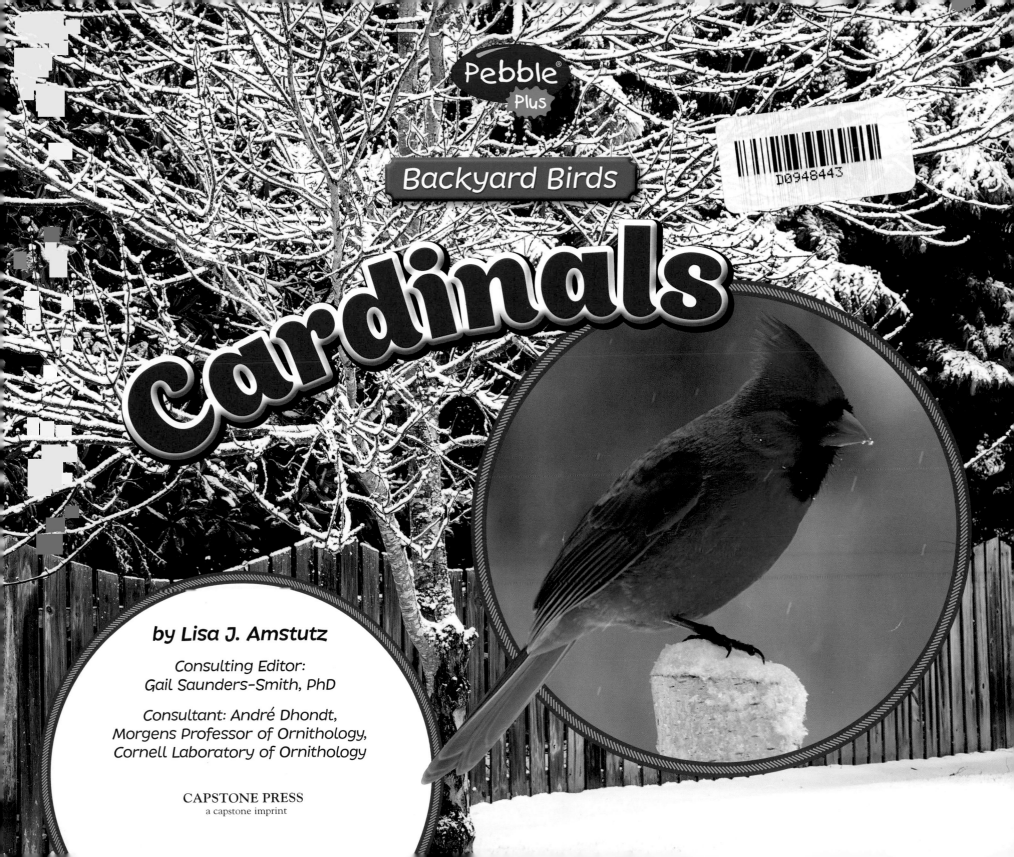

Pebble® Plus

Backyard Birds

Cardinals

by Lisa J. Amstutz

Consulting Editor:
Gail Saunders-Smith, PhD

Consultant: André Dhondt,
Morgens Professor of Ornithology,
Cornell Laboratory of Ornithology

CAPSTONE PRESS
a capstone imprint

Pebble Plus is published by Capstone Press,
1710 Roe Crest Drive, North Mankato, Minnesota 56003
www.capstonepub.com

Library of Congress Cataloging-in-Publication Data
Amstutz, Lisa J., author.
 Cardinals / by Lisa J. Amstutz.
    pages cm. — (Pebble plus. Backyard birds.)
 Summary: "Simple text and full-color photographs introduce northern cardinals"—Provided
by publisher.
 Audience: Age 5-7.
 Audience: K to grade 3.
 Includes bibliographical references and index.
 ISBN 978-1-4914-6107-5 (library binding)
 ISBN 978-1-4914-6111-2 (paperback)
 ISBN 978-1-4914-6115-0 (eBook PDF)
1. Cardinals (Birds)—Juvenile literature. I. Title.
 QL696.P2438A47 2016
 598.8'83—dc23   2015001437

Editorial Credits
Elizabeth R. Johnson, editor; Bobbie Nuytten, designer;
Svetlana Zhurkin, media researcher; Tori Abraham, production specialist

Photo Credits
Dreamstime: Paul Roedding, 5; Newscom: WLP/Douglas Graham, 13; Shutterstock: Andrew
Williams, 11, Anne Kitzman, 15, bee67, 4 (back) and throughout, Bonnie Taylor Barry, 7, 19,
Bruce MacQueen, 9, Darryl Brooks, cover (back), 1 (back), 2—3, 24, Ivan Kuzmin, 17, Oleg
Iatsun, 4 (front) and throughout, Steven Russell Smith Photos, cover (inset), 1 (inset), 21

Note to Parents and Teachers

The Backyard Birds set supports national curriculum standards for science related to
life science and ecosystems. This book describes and illustrates northern cardinals.
The images support early readers in understanding the text. The repetition of words
and phrases helps early readers learn new words. This book also introduces early
readers to subject-specific vocabulary words, which are defined in the Glossary
section. Early readers may need assistance to read some words and to use the Table of
Contents, Glossary, Read More, Internet Sites, Critical Thinking Using the Common
Core, and Index sections of the book.

Printed in the United States of America in North Mankato, Minnesota.
032015   008823CGF15

Table of Contents

All About Cardinals

A northern cardinal perches in a tree. It sings a cheery song. *Birdie, birdie, birdie!* These colorful birds are easy to spot.

Cardinals are 8 to 9 inches
(20 to 23 centimeters) long.
Males are bright red.
Females are light brown
with hints of red.

Cardinals eat seeds, fruit, and insects. They like to visit bird feeders. Sunflower seeds are a favorite treat.

Where Cardinals Live

Cardinals live in parts of North and Central America. They can be found in forests, fields, and towns.

Cardinals make nests in trees
and shrubs. The female shapes
twigs into a cup with her feet.
She lines the nest with leaves,
bark, and grass.

The Life of a Cardinal

The female lays two to five speckled eggs in spring. She sits on them to keep them warm.

The chicks hatch in about 12 days. They open their mouths to beg for food. Their parents feed them insects.

The chicks grow fast.

They leave the nest after 10 days.

They learn to fly and find food.

It is fun to watch
these lively birds.
Look for cardinals
in your backyard!

Cardinal Range

■ Year-round

Glossary

chick—a young bird

hatch—to break out of an egg

hint—a tiny amount; a trace

nest—a place to lay eggs and bring up young

perch—to sit or stand on a branch or on the edge of something, often high up

speckled—marked with small spots or patches of color

Read More

Alderfer, Jonathan. *National Geographic Kids Bird Guide of North America*. Washington, D.C.: National Geographic, 2013.

Kurki, Kim. *National Wildlife Federation's World of Birds: A Beginner's Guide*. New York: Black Dog & Leventhal Publishers, 2014.

Mara, Wil. *Cardinals*. Backyard Safari. New York: Cavendish Square Publishing, 2014.

Internet Sites

FactHound offers a safe, fun way to find Internet sites related to this book. All of the sites on FactHound have been researched by our staff.

Here's all you do:

Visit *www.facthound.com*

Type in this code: 9781491461075

Super-cool stuff! Check out projects, games and lots more at **www.capstonekids.com**

Critical Thinking
Using the Common Core

1. What kinds of food do cardinals like to eat? (Key Ideas and Details)

2. Look at the picture on page 17. Why are the chicks' mouths open? (Integration of Knowledge and Ideas)

Index

Word Count: 177
Grade: 1
Early-Intervention Level: 13